# Another Look at Six Myths in The Lost Cause

By Richard Lee Montgomery

The
Scuppernong Press
Wake Forest, NC

*Another Look at Six Myths in The Lost Cause*

First Printing

The Scuppernong Press
PO Box 1724
Wake Forest, NC 27588
www.scuppernongpress.com

Cover and book design by Frank B. Powell, III

International Standard Book Number ISBN 978-0-9898399-0-7

Library of Congress Control Number: 2013947772

*History books, the media, school systems and on, and on, and on, abound in falsehoods and inaccuracies of Confederate and Southern history. Here are but a few fictional teachings which are presented today as true.*

# Table of Contents

# The War Between the States of 1861-1864 Was Fought Over Slavery

This is simply not true. The North fought the war over money. Plain and simple. When the South started Secession, Lincoln was asked in March 1861 by a newspaper at a Virginia Compromise Delegation, "Why not let the South go in peace?" Abraham Lincoln replied, "Let the South go? Let the South go! Where then shall we gain our revenues?"[1] This is Abraham Lincoln alluding to the fact the South paid 85 percent of the tax burden of this nation at that time. Sensing total financial ruin for the North, Lincoln waged war on the South.

Lincoln

The South fought the War to repel Northern aggression and invasion. Even Charles Dickens saw this in 1862 by saying, "The Northern onslaught upon slavery was no more than a piece

Dickens

of specious humbug designed to conceal its desire for economic control of the Southern states."[2] Important to the issue at hand is what Abraham Lincoln said in his speech to the United States House of Representatives January 12, 1848, concerning the war with Mexico, "Any people, anywhere, being inclined and having the power, have the right to rise up and shake off the existing government, and form a new one that suits them better. This is a most valuable, a most sacred

---

[1] Frank H. Alfriend, *The Life of Jefferson Davis* (Cincinnati: Caxton Publishing House, 1868), 201.
[2] Iain C. Martin, *The Quotable American Civil War*, (Lyons Press, 2008), 119.

right; a right which we hope and believe is to liberate the world."[3] If only Lincoln had still felt this way before he made the decision to send Union troops to Ft. Sumter in Charleston Harbor, South Carolina, which arrived April 11, 1861. Now back to the central issue. If the War of 1861-1865 was fought over slavery, why were there citizens, and more importantly, military leaders in the North who still had slaves?

Grant

The first one that comes to mind is Major General Ulysses S. Grant who was chosen by Lincoln to command his army and this Grant did successfully. Here is the confusion, at least in my mind. In the summer of 1861 Grant, then the colonel of the Twenty-first Illinois Regiment of Infantry, made the comment, "I have no doubt in the world that the sole object is the restoration of the Union. I will say further, though, that I am a Democrat — every man in my regiment is a Democrat — and whenever I shall be convinced that this war has for its object anything else than what I have mentioned, or that the government designs using its soldiers to execute the purposes of the abolitionists, I pledge you my honor as a man and a soldier that I will not only resign my commission, but will carry my sword to the other side, and cast my lot with that people"[4] Grant's motive for fighting the Confederacy was not to free the slaves.

Another one which comes to mind is General William T. Sherman. In a letter to General Henry W. Halleck, September 14, 1864, Sherman conveyed, "I am honest in my belief that it is not fair to my men to count negros as equals. Let us capture negros, of course, and use them to the best advantage"[5]

Sherman

Sherman expressed his opinions when he wrote to his wife in 1860, "All the congresses on earth can't make the negro anything else than what he is; he must be subject to the white man."[6] "Two such races can-

[3]Roy P. Basler, *The Collected Works of Abraham Lincoln*, Volume 1, (Rutgers University Press, New Brunswick, New Jersey, 1953), 431-42.

[4]Matthew Carey Jr., *The Democratic Speaker's Hand Book*, (Cincinnati: Miami Print and Pub Company, 1868), 33.

[5]Christopher Dorsey, *A Call to Arms: The Realities of Military Service for African Americans During the Civil War*, (Backintyme, 2007), 50.

not live in harmony save as master and slave."[7] In a letter to his anti-slavery brother-in-law about plans to bring his family to Louisiana, Sherman crassly joked about becoming a slave master himself. Making light of the problems he anticipated in keeping white servants, he wrote that his wife Ellen "will have to wait on herself or buy a nigger."[8]

The War Between the States was not fought over slavery. Wouldn't you think that if it was that, Lincoln would have freed the slaves in the North? According to the "Emancipation Proclamation," January 1, 1863, only the slaves in the South were freed, that "all persons held as slaves" within the rebellious areas "are, and henceforward shall be free." This was an "executive order" to free all slaves of the Confederate States of American but it was not about freeing slaves in the United States of America.

If the War Between the States was about freeing slaves, why did they (the North) not free their slaves at the beginning of the war and not during the war or after the war? Ninety-nine percent of the soldiers who fought under the Stars and Bars never owned any slaves, but fought for states' rights, against Northern aggression. It was not until well into the supposed war to free slaves that the issue of slavery was brought up and then the North used it as justification for the continued aggression of the South.

Lincoln knew if he sought to free the slaves in the Northern states, there would be a rebellion in those states. Lincoln even expressed his fear by saying, "I would do it if I were not afraid that half the officers would fling down their arms and three more states would rise."[9]

Before Lincoln's fourth debate with Douglas in Charleston, Illinois, September 18, 1858, Democrats held up a banner that read "Negro equality" with a picture of a white man, a negro woman and a mulatto child. At this debate Lincoln went further than before in denying the charge that he was an abolitionist, saying that,

*"I am not, nor ever have been, in favor of bringing about in any way the social and political equality of the white and black races, that I am not nor*

---

[6]M. A. DeWolfe Howe, *Home Letters of General Sherman*, (New York: C. Scribner's Sons, 1909), 176-177.
[7]Ibid., 178.
[8]Lloyd Lewis, *Sherman: Fighting Prophet*, (University of Nebraska Press, 1932), 120.
[9]Edward Lillie Pierce, *Memoir and Letters of Charles Sumner*, Volume 4, (Boston: Roberts Brothers, 1894), 83.

ever have been in favor of making voters or jurors of negroes, nor of qualifying them to hold office, nor to intermarry with white people; and I will say in addition to this that there is a physical difference between the white and black races which I believe will forever forbid the two races living together on terms of social and political equality. And in as much as they cannot so live, while they do remain together there must be the position of superior and inferior, and I as much as any other man am in favor of having the superior position assigned to the white race. I say upon this occasion I do not perceive that because the white man is to have the superior position the negro should be denied everything."[10]

Those are not the markings of someone who is seeking to free a people in order for them to have "life, liberty and the pursuit of happiness." In fact, it might be of interest for the people of the United States to know that Mr. Lincoln was not only *not* an abolitionist but that he had a vested interest in deporting all blacks to western Africa (Liberia) for colonization. This was Abraham Lincoln's solution to the slavery problem. According to Lerone Bennett Jr.'s book entitled *Forced into Glory: Abraham Lincoln's White Dream*, Bennett stated that ideally Lincoln wanted to create an all-white nation.[11] In 1855, Lincoln became a member of the Illinois Colonization Society and in 1857; he became a "manager," which sought to use state tax funds to deport the small number of free blacks living in Illinois out of the state. Perhaps, it should have already been stated that the state of Illinois amended its constitution in 1848 to prohibit the immigration of black people into the state, an amendment which Lincoln supported. Maybe this is why there were so few blacks in the state.

**The War Between the States was not fought over slavery.**

---

[10]*Abraham Lincoln: Speeches and Writings*, 1832-1858, (New York: Library of America, 1989), 636-637.
[11]Lerone Bennett Jr., *Forced into Glory: Abraham Lincoln's White Dream*, (Johnson Publishing Company, Inc, 2007), 513-514.

# The Confederate Battle Flag Was Flown On Slave Ships

Again, just not true. At no time were there ever any flags of the Confederacy flying over a slave ship. Nor did the Confederacy own or operate any slave ships. When the slave traders of England, Holland and Portugal brought slaves to the United States from Africa, they were brought to the Northern states, not to the Southern states. From the North the slaves were transported to the South, transported in ships from the Northern states of Massachusetts, Rhode Island, New York, New Jersey and Delaware under flags from other countries or the United States flag.

In fact, for the North, the slave trading industry was big business, especially the New England area. This slave trade market came to be known as the "Triangular Trade." The North traded their rum to African slave owners for their slaves and then traded most of the slaves to South America or to the West Indies for molasses. Then the molasses was manufactured into rum in the North and the process was started all over again. Most believe only five percent of the African slaves ever reached the United States. Sad to say, slavery was a legal institution in this country for more than 200 years.

The name of the first slave ship built in the English colonies was the *Desire*, launched from Marblehead, Massachusetts, in 1637. Historical documentation shows "The first negroes brought into the colony, so far as we know, came in the ship *Desire*, Captain Peirce, February 26, 1637-38, who brought home some cotton and tobacco and negroes from the West Indies."[12]

---

[12]Charles Deane, *The Connection Of Massachusetts With Slavery And The Slave Trade*, (Worcester, Mass: Charles Hamilton,1886), 18.

Hopkins

The slave ship *Sally*, was owned by Nicholas Brown and Company, a Providence, Rhode Island, merchant firm run by four brothers, Nicholas, John, Joseph and Moses Brown. Its career only lasted one year from 1764-1765. Its sole use was for slave transportation and it flew under the United States flag. There is an interesting twist to rest of the story concerning the slave ship *Sally*. The master of the vessel was Esek Hopkins[13] from September 1764 to December 1765, who later became the first commander-in-chief of the United States Navy.

In 1850, the slave ship *Martha*, a New York registered ship was captured by the USS *Perry* when about to embark from the southern coast of Africa with 1,800 slaves. The captain paid his bail and then escaped. The slave ship *Hope*, harbored out of Newport, Rhode Island, was confiscated for violations of slave trading in 1795. Its owner was John Brown who was a state representative.[14]

The slave ship *Nightingale*,[15] owned and operated by the City of Boston, Massachusetts,[16] was built in Portsmouth, New Hampshire, in 1851. Its original use was a tea clipper and then a slave ship. As a slave ship, she was captured in 1861 by the USS *Saratoga*

*Nightingale*

in Africa. Then she was used as a supply ship and carried coal, while supporting the Union Navy ships blockading the Confederate States of America. Following this conflict, the *Nightingale* went on to a long career in the Arctic exploration and merchant trading business before sinking in the North Atlantic in 1893. But throughout its career, it flew under the United States flag.

---

[13]Joseph E. Inikori, *The Atlantic Slave Trade: Effects on Economies, Societies and Peoples in Africa, the Americas, and Europe*, (Duke University Press Books, 1992), 224.
[14]Jay Coughtry, *The Notorious Triangle: Rhode Island and the African Slave Trade*, (Philadelphia, 1981), 214–215.
[15]*Some Ships of the Clipper Ship Era: Their Builders, Owners, and Captains*, (Boston, MA: Printed for the State Street Trust Company, 1913), 37.
[16]Arthur H. Jennings, Chairman, *The Gray Book*, (Gray Book Committee S.C.V., By Authority, and Under Auspices of the Sons of Confederate Veterans, 1920), 16.

There were many other slave ships which were built in the North with a good number of them making their harbor homes in the North. In fact, many of the leading slave merchants in the North were leading citizens, prominent families who became very wealthy on the slave trade. Bostonian Peter Fanueil (1700-1743) was one of the wealthiest men in the Colonies. He was a philanthropist and a slave trader who shipped slaves to the West Indies and with his money funded the building of Faneuil Hall in Boston.[17] When he died he left his fortune, including five slaves, with his brother and sister.

Fanueil

Another slave trader from Massachusetts was Isaac Royall Sr. (1672-1739), who was also a rum distiller and wealthy merchant. He was born in Maine and later moved to Medford, Massachusetts, when he was three years old. As a business merchant (shipping industry) he became

Royall

very wealthy participating in the Atlantic Slave Trade. From Salem, Massachusetts, John Cabot (1680-1742) was a highly successful merchant operating a fleet of privateers carrying opium, rum, and slaves.

From Rhode Island was James DeWolf (1764-1837), nicknamed "Captain Jim," who would become a senator (1821-1825) from Bristol, Rhode Island. He became captain of a ship before he was 20 and engaged in commercial ventures, including trading in slaves, with Cuba and other West Indian islands and from 1769-1820, the DeWolfs were the nation's leading slave traders. It has been said when he died, he was the second richest[18] person in the country.

One of the more successful business families of colonial America was the Brown family of Providence, Rhode Island, who were also slave traders. At least six of them: James and his brother Obadiah and James's four sons, Nicholas, John, Joseph and Moses ran one of the largest slave-trading businesses in New England, and brought them great wealth. "When James Brown sent the *Mary* to Africa in 1736, he launched Providence

---

[17]Walter Donald Kennedy, *Myths of American Slavery*, (Pelican Publishing; 1St Edition, 2003), 103.
[18]Thomas Norman DeWolf, *Inheriting the Trade: A Northern Family Confronts Its Legacy as the Largest Slave-Trading Dynasty in U.S. History* (Beacon Press, 2008), 117-118.

**DeWolf**

into the Negro traffic and laid the foundation for the Brown fortune. From this year until 1790, the Browns played a commanding role in the New England slave trade."[19] Because of Nicholas Brown's gift of $5,000 to Rhode Island College, its name was changed to Brown University in 1804.[20] It was a well know fact that Massachusetts and Rhode Island were the major slave trading colonies in New England with Boston and Newport as the major ports for slave ships. More than that, it was the North which was the foundation to the slave trading industry in North America and obviously, the flag that was used was not the Confederate Battle Flag.

Even today a person doesn't have to look far to find Northern institution of antiquity which isn't tainted by slavery. The president of Yale, Ezra Stiles, imported slaves while in office.[21] Brown University is named for the Brown brothers, Nicholas, John, Joseph and Moses, manufacturers and traders who shipped salt, lumber, meat and slaves. Even after slavery was outlawed in the North, ships out of New England continued to carry thousands of Africans to the American South. Some 156,000 slaves were brought to the United States in the period 1801-08, almost all of them on ships which sailed from New England ports which had recently outlawed slavery. Rhode Island slavers alone imported an average of 6,400 Africans annually into the U.S. in the years 1805 and 1806. The financial base of New England's antebellum manufacturing boom was money it had made in shipping. And that shipping money was largely acquired directly or indirectly from slavery, whether by importing Africans to the Americas, transporting slave-grown cotton to England, or hauling Pennsylvania wheat and Rhode Island rum to the slave-labor colonies of the Caribbean. Northerners profited from slavery in many ways, right up to the eve of the War Between the States under the flags of the North.

All in all, slave ships were built in the North — slave ships were harbored in the Northern ports. Again, even when slavery was illegal, there

---

[19]Lorenzo Johnston Greene, *The Negro in Colonial New England*, 1620-1776 (N.Y.: Columbia University Press, 1942), 30.
[20]*The Sesquicentennial of Brown University*, 1764-1914 (Printed By The University, 1915), 172.
[21]Edgar J. McManus, *Black Bondage in the North* (N.Y.: Syracuse University Printing, 2002), 19.

were slave traders in the North. The flags of these ships represented the nation they were from, including "Old Glory" of North America. But the Confederate Battle Flag was not flown on any slave ships.

The *New York Times* published an article November 3, 2010, written by Adam Goodheart and entitled "November 4, 1860"

*"If you had risen early on that Sunday morning, you probably would have ventured out to marvel at the wreckage left by the past night's storm. Trees had toppled; shop signs lay smashed on the cobblestones. All along the wharves of lower Manhattan, ships had lost spars and rigging.*

*"And on the harbor's restless water, a three-masted merchant vessel tossed and bucked at her mooring lines. If you drew close, you might still have caught a whiff of the distinctive stench that every well-traveled mariner in that day and age knew: the reek of close-packed bodies, of human misery, of captivity and death.*

*"She was the slaver* Erie, *and she had recently come to New York as a captive herself. A U.S. naval vessel, patrolling for ships engaged in the illicit trade, had seized her off the mouth of the Congo River. Flinging open the hatches to the cargo hold, the officers saw a dim tangle of bodies moving in the darkness, packed so tightly that they seemed almost a single tormented soul. Nearly 900 Africans — half of them children — had been stripped naked and forced below decks at the height of equatorial summer, aboard a vessel barely more than 100 feet long. Just a few days into their weeks-long voyage, a witness later recalled, "their sufferings were really agonizing, and … the stench arising from their unchecked filthiness was absolutely startling." Even after their rescue, dozens died in a matter of days."*

It might seem odd today the American government was freeing slaves across the Atlantic while zealously protecting the "property rights" of slaveholders closer to home. Not long after Congress abolished slave importation in 1808, however, U.S. and British naval vessels had begun policing the African coasts and the waters of the Caribbean, occasionally even bringing the captains and crews back to stand trial under federal law. (The freed captives, no matter where in Africa they had come from, were set ashore in Liberia, often to be set to work there in conditions little better than slavery.) It was one of many such hypocrisies, born of political compromise most Americans in 1860 took for granted.

Like the majority of slavers at the time, the *Erie* had been bound for Cuba, where importation was still legal. Her human cargo might have fetched somewhere between half a million and a million dollars there

— depending, of course, on how many captives perished during the crossing. A mortality rate of one in five or so was taken for granted in the trade, but the *Erie's* record on past voyages had been even worse than this horrific average. Still, enormous profits were to be made. The slaver's New England-born captain, Nathaniel Gordon, had purchased the Africans with kegs of whiskey. He was now a prisoner in the Eldridge Street jail.

The *Erie* was no stranger to New York. It was, indeed, her home port, as it was of many such vessels. Nearly 100 clandestine — or barely clandestine — slaving voyages had set out from the city over the past 18 months alone. Notorious traders in human flesh hung out their shingles in front of offices on Pearl and Beaver Streets downtown, scarcely bothering to camouflage themselves as legitimate shipping merchants.

Slavery was in the lifeblood of the metropolis. An editorial in that same Sunday's *New York Herald* warned local citizens against electing a candidate like Lincoln who might interfere with the institution in the American South. Slave-grown cotton was one of the greatest sources of the city's wealth, the paper pointed out. Rashly frightening the slave states out of the Union would be "like killing the goose that laid the golden eggs."

The next day, in U.S. district court, the *Erie* was officially confiscated by the government and ordered to be sold. The slave ship went up for auction a few weeks later at the Atlantic Dock in Brooklyn, sold for $7,550, and was lost to history.

Her captain's fate would take much longer for the courts — and the incoming president to decide.[22]

It is a fact slavery in North America never achieved the scale it did in the Caribbean or South America. But of the approximately twelve million Africans transported to America by the mid-nineteenth century, six hundred thousand (or five percent) came to mainland North America, and about one hundred thousand (or one percent) were carried in Rhode Island ships. Slavery would come to an end in the 1860s, but right up to its end, the slave trade was alive and well in the North. The slave trade was a giant institution in the North and just because it was illegal,

---

[22]Adam Goodheart November 3, 2010. *New York Times.* or http://opinionator.blogs. nytimes. com/ 2010/11/03/a-slave-ship-in-new-york/

**1st National (Stars and Bars)**

**Confederate Battle Flag**

doesn't mean it was not happening.

Any easy study will show the First National Flag of the Confederacy was known as "The Stars and Bars." It's important to say the stars represent the first seven states of the Confederacy: South Carolina, Mississippi, Florida, Alabama, Georgia, Louisiana and Texas and; the bars represent the judiciary, legislative, and executive branches of government. It was never used to fly over any slave ships.

The one flag which was used by Confederate troops which receives the most criticism today is the "rebel flag." It does need to be noted this was called the "Confederate Battle Flag." Like the National Flag, the Battle Flag was never used to fly over any slave ships. The Battle Flag was the soldier's flag.

From 1641, when Massachusetts first legalized slavery, until 1865, when the Confederate struggle for Southern independence ended, slavery was a legal institution in America which lasted more than 224 years. The Confederate National Flags and the Battle Flag flew for four years of those 224 years. It was the United States Flag the slave first saw, and it was the United States Flag which flew on the mast of New England slave ships as they brought their human cargo to this country. It is clear, that those who attack the Confederate Flag as a reminder of slavery are overlooking the most guilty and hateful of all reminders of American slavery, the United States Flag.

*The Confederate Battle Flag was not flown on slave ships.*

*Another Look At Six Myths In The Lost Cause — Richard Lee Montgomery*

# ☞ Myth # 3

## The Confederate "Battle Flag" Represented the "Southern Nation"

Not true. While the Southern Battle Flag was carried into battle, the Confederate States of America had three different National Flags during the course of the war of Northern aggression.

The First National Flag of the Confederacy was known by the people of the South as the "Stars and Bars." It flew from March 4, 1861, to May 1, 1863. While there is debate as to the author for its design, the Alabama legislature has declared the inspiration came from the Austrian Flag and was designed by the Prussian Artist Nicola Marschall in Marion, Alabama. However, Orren Randolph Smith of North Carolina also claimed the design and the United Confederate Veterans found in his favor in a 1915 report. Both men may be entitled to claim the honor.[23]

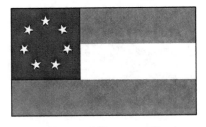

1st National (Stars and Bars)

The "Stars and Bars" flag was adopted March 4, 1861 in Montgomery, Alabama and raised over the dome of the first Confederate Capitol. Also, as a side note, Marschall designed the Confederate Army uniform.

The Confederacy changed the "Stars and Bars" on four different occasions. Each time there was a change, new states where added to the "stars." The first "Stars and Bars" had seven stars which represent South

---

[23]Edgar Erskine Hume, *The German Artist Who Designed the Confederate Flag and Uniform* (*The American-German Review*, August, 1940), 39.
Devereaux D. Cannon, Jr., *The Flags of the Confederacy*, (St. Lukes Press and Broadfoot Publishing, 1988), 10-12.

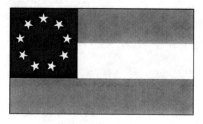

1st National with nine stars                    1st National with eleven stars

Carolina, Mississippi, Florida, Alabama, Georgia, Louisiana and Texas.
The second "Stars and Bars" added the states (stars) of Louisiana and
Virginia to make it a total number of nine stars. The third "Stars and
Bars" added North Carolina and Tennessee, making it eleven stars and
then finally, the fourth "Stars and Bars" added Kentucky and Missouri
with a final count of thirteen stars (states). The "Stars and Bars" was the
first national flag. But this flag was changed due to the resemblance of
the United States Flag.

The Second National Flag design was specified by the Confederate
Congress to be a white field "with the union (now used as the battle flag)
to be a square of two-thirds the width of the flag, having the ground

2nd National Flag (Stainless Banner)

red; thereupon a broad saltier of
blue, bordered with white, and
emblazoned with mullets or
five-pointed stars, correspond-
ing in number to that of the
Confederate States."[24]

This Second National Flag
was approved by both houses
and became official on May 1,
1863. It was first used to cover
the coffin of Lieutenant General Thomas Jonathan "Stonewall" Jackson,[25]
who was wounded at the Battle of Chancellorsville on May 2 and died
of pneumonia on May 10. His coffin was draped with the new Second
National Flag while it was placed in the chamber of the House of Repre-

---

[24]J. Kellogg, *Confederate Women of Arkansas In The Civil War: 1861-1865*, (The United Confederate Veterans of Arkansas, 1907), 179.
[25]Sarah Nicholas Randolph, *The Life of General Thomas J. Jackson* (Philadelphia: J. B. Lippincott & Co., 1876), 350.

sentatives on May 12. From this event, the Second National Flag was often called the "Stonewall Jackson flag."

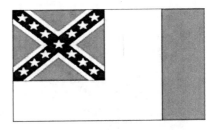

3rd National Flag

This flag was also nicknamed the "Stainless Banner" because of its pure white field. At first, the reaction to the Second National Flag was favorable, but over time it became criticized for being "too white." Certainly it was used as the flag on government buildings and forts and even was designated by the secretary of the navy as the official naval jack. But the reaction by the Confederate Army, as a whole, did not take to the new flag. When the "Stainless Banner" was sent to the army camps, it was trumped by the "Stars and Bars," the First National Flag. Even as late as the Battle of Gettysburg, there were units in the Army of Northern Virginia continuing to use the "Stars and Bars." In large part, the Army of Northern Virginia units who received the new flags cut off the white field and flew only the small battle flag when on active service. Soldiers in the Western theater, however, apparently took to the new flag more than those in the East. But why, when looking at the big picture, was the Second National Flag not received positively throughout the war? Primarily, it resembled the look of a flag of truce, especially when the flag was limp on the flagpole when there was no wind. This appearance would bring confusion to both sides. So another change to the national flag was in order.

The Third National Flag was proposed by Major Arthur L. Rogers and was adopted March 4, 1865 as the flag of the Confederacy. It too had a nickname, "the Blood Stained Banner." According to Rogers, the white symbolized purity and innocence, and the red fortitude and courage. The cross of St. Andrew indicated descent from British stock, while the red bar was taken from the French flag, as many other Southerners were descended from French stock. But the destiny of this national flag would have a short life span, because the war for Southern Independence would come to an end May 9, 1865, two weeks after the Third National Flag was adopted. It is unlikely the Third National Flag ever flew over any Confederate troops or civilian agencies. Confederate General Bradley T. Johnson wrote, "I never saw this flag, nor have I seen a man who

**Confederate Battle Flag**

did see it, or who saw a man who did see it."[26]

In simple terms, while history records there were three different National Flags of the Confederacy, historians continue to teach it was the "Stars and Bars" which was the flag which represented the Southern Nation most.

Perhaps the most recognizable flag of the Confederacy was the Battle Flag, but it was never the national flag for the Confederate States of America. It was used by Confederate troops throughout the war and was often called the "Southern Cross" or the cross of St. Andrew. This was the soldier's flag, especially used by the Army of Northern Virginia and the Army of Tennessee.

The reason for this flag to have been created was because of what happened during the first major conflict between the "Blue" and the "Gray." During the battle of First Manassas or as the Yankees called it, "Bull Run," General P.G.T. Beauregard had trouble distinguishing the United States flag from the First National Flag, the "Stars and Bars." It was not until the wind picked up that he was able to identify the proper flags.

After this battle, General Gustave T. Beauregard wrote, "I resolve to have our flag changed or to adopt for command a battle flag, which would be entirely different from any state or federal flag."[27] Thus, the flag with the Saint Andrews cross was selected. The design of the flag had thirteen white stars on a blue cross which represented the thirteen states of the Confederacy: Virginia, North Carolina, South Carolina, Tennessee, Georgia, Florida, Alabama, Mississippi, Louisiana,

**Beauregard**

---

[26] *Southern Historical Society Papers*, Volume 24, 1876, 118.

[27] Ray Adkins, *One Foggy Morning in Barbourville, Kentucky* (CreateSpace Independent Publishing Platform, 2008), 234.

Arkansas, Texas, Missouri and Kentucky. But it must be reiterated that this flag was the soldier's flag and was never used as a flag to represent the Confederacy as a national flag. To the true Southerner, the flag represents heritage and respect for our ancestors, nothing more, nothing less.

*Simply put, the Confederate Battle Flag did not represent the Southern Nation because it was the soldier's battle flag.*

# ☞ Myth # 4

## Only The North Had Men of Color in Their Ranks

History shows that this just is not true. There were many blacks, those who were slaves fought alongside with their white owners. There were blacks who were free and of their own will, joined the

Winbush

Edgerton

Confederate Army to fight for their beloved Southern home. But just as important, there were other ethnic groups who fought as well. The Oriental, Mexican, Spanish and the Native American Indians fought with pride for the South.

Years following the war of 1861-1865, many men of color became members of the Sons of the Confederate Veterans (SCV). Notable black members include Nelson W. Winbush, a retired educator,[28] Major Willie Levi Casey Jr., a U.S. Army officer,[29] and H. K. Edgerton (associate member), a former president of an NAACP chapter.[30] Other notable members have been President Harry S. Truman, Hank Williams Jr., country music star; Clint Eastwood, actor and director; R. Michael Givens, film director; and Patrick J. Buchanan, political commentator.

Eastwood

---

[28]"In Defense of His Confederate Pride," *St. Petersburg Times*, October 2007, retrieved March 22, 2011.
[29]"Laura Moyer, Rebel Re-Enactor With A Cause," *The Free Lance-Star*, June 30, 2002.
[30]*Black Southerner Marching To D.C., Seeks Respect For Confederate Flag*, Sons of Confederate Veterans.

Today, there continues to be a barrage of attacks on the idea that a person of color, especially black, would ever be willing to fight for the Confederacy, since they were all slaves and were treated brutally by their owners. But the fact of history tells us a different story than what is being taught in schools and written by the media. There were men of color who took pride in their heritage and because of that, they did whatever task was given them, in order to serve in the Confederate Army.

## Negroes (Blacks) in Confederacy

One of those men was a black Confederate soldier by the name of Louis Napoleon Nelson, the grandfather of Nelson W. Winbush, who is a black advocate and member of the Sons of the Confederate Veterans.

He speaks of his grandfather as "a private in Co. M, 7th Tennessee Cavalry of the Confederate Army during the War Between the States. Private Nelson was a slave at the start of the war. He began his military service as a cook, then a rifleman and finally a chaplain." Nelson also stated his grandfather rode with General Nathan Bedford Forrest.

**Nelson**

In his book, Ervin L. Jordan writes, "Some Northerners considered it laughable that Southerners, who had long proclaimed the incompetence of blacks in any intellectual activity, would even discuss the subject. I do not believe that one thinking Southern man ... has any more idea of arming his Negroes," commented one writer in the *Atlantic Monthly*. Nevertheless, eyewitness accounts by Union officers are plausible evidence of African-American participation on the battlefields of Virginia for the Confederacy. New York soldiers on patrol from Newport News were attacked near Newmarket Bridge by Confederate Calvary and a group of 700 armed blacks on December 1861. The Unionists killed six of the blacks before retreating; officers later swore out an affidavit stating they were attacked by blacks and complained: "If they (the rebels) fight us with Negroes, why should we not fight them

**Forrest**

**Wesley**

with Negroes, too? ... Let us fight the devil with fire."[31]

Charles H. Wesley, a distinguished black historian who lived from 1891 to 1987, wrote "The Employment of Negroes as Soldiers in the Confederate Army," in the *Journal of Negro History* (1919). He says, "The loyalty of the slave while the master was away with the fighting forces of the Confederacy has been the making of many orators of an earlier day, echoes of which we often hear in the present. The Negroes were not only loyal in remaining at home and doing their duty but also in offering themselves for actual service in the Confederate army. Believing their land invaded by hostile foes, they were more than willing under the guidance of misguided Southerners to offer themselves for the service of actual warfare. So that during the early days of the war, Negroes who volunteered were received into the fighting forces by the rebelling States, and particularly during those years in which the North was academically debating the advisability of arming the Negro.[32]

Wesley goes on to say, an observer in Charleston at the outbreak of the war noted the preparation for war, and called particular attention to "the thousand Negroes who, so far from inclining to insurrections, were grinning from ear to ear at the prospect of shooting the Yankees." In the same city, one of the daily papers stated on January 2, 150 free colored men had gratuitously offered their services to hasten the work of throwing up redoubts along the coast. At Nashville, Tennessee, April, 1861, a company of free Negroes offered their services to the Confederate government and at Memphis a recruiting office was opened. The legislature of Tennessee authorized Governor Harris on June 28, 1861, to receive into the state military service all male persons of color between the ages of fifteen and fifty. These soldiers would receive eight dollars a month with clothing and rations. The sheriff of each county was required to report the names of these persons and in case the number of persons tendering their services was not sufficient to meet the needs of the county, the sheriff was empowered to impress as many persons as were needed. In the same state, a procession of several hundred colored men marching through the streets attracted attention. They marched under the com-

---

[31]Ervin L. Jordan, *Confederates and Afro-Yankees in Civil War Virginia* (University of Virginia, 1995), 222.

[32]Charles H. Wesley, *The Employment of Negroes As Soldiers in the Confederate Army* (*The Journal of Negro History* Volume IV, July, No. 3, 1919), 241-242.

mand of Confederate officers and carried shovels, axes and blankets. The observer adds, "they were brimful of patriotism, shouting for Jeff Davis and singing war songs." A paper in Lynchburg, Virginia, commenting on the enlistment of 70 free Negroes to fight for the defense of the state, concluded with "three cheers for the patriotic Negroes of Lynchburg."

Two weeks after the firing on Fort Sumter, several companies of volunteers of color passed through Augusta on their way to Virginia to engage in actual war. Sixteen well-drilled companies of volunteers and one Negro company from Nashville composed this group. In November of the same year, a military review was held in New Orleans. Twenty-eight thousand troops passed before Governor Moore, General Lowell and General Ruggles. The line of march covered more than seven miles in length. It is said one regiment comprised 1,400 free colored men. *The Baltimore Traveler* commenting on arming Negroes at Richmond, said: "Contrabands who have recently come within the Federal lines at Williamsport, report that all the able-bodied men in that vicinity are being taken to Richmond, formed into regiments, and armed for the defense of that city."[33]

Greeley

Even the notable Horace Greeley, the founder and editor of *The New York Tribune*, perhaps America's most influential newspaper from the 1840s to the 1870s tells us, "For more than two years, Negroes had been extensively employed in belligerent operations by the Confederacy. They had been embodied and drilled as rebel soldiers and had paraded with white troops at a time when this would not have been tolerated in the armies of the Union."[34]

Even the chief inspector of the Union Sanitary Commission, Dr. Lewis Steiner, reported he saw about 3,000 well-armed black Confederate soldiers in Stonewall Jackson's army in Frederick, Maryland, and that those soldiers were "manifestly an integral portion of the Southern Confederate Army." Dr. Steiner reported, Wednesday, September 10 — At four o'clock this morning the rebel army began to

---

[33]Charles H. Wesley, *The Employment of Negroes As Soldiers in the Confederate Army* (*The Journal of Negro History* Volume IV, July, No. 3, 1919), 244-245.

[34]Horace Greely, *The American Conflict*, Vol. 2 (Hartford: O. D. Case & Company, 1867), 524.

move from our town, Jackson's force taking the advance. The movement continued until eight o'clock P.M., occupying sixteen hours. The most liberal calculations could not give them more than 64,000 men. Over 3,000 Negroes must be included in this number. These were clad in all kinds of uniforms, not only in cast-off or captured United States uniforms, but in coats with Southern buttons, State buttons, etc. These were shabby, but not shabbier or seedier than those worn by white men in rebel ranks. Most of the Negroes had arms, rifles, muskets, sabers, bowie-knives, dirks, etc. They were supplied, in many instances, with knapsacks, haversacks, canteens, etc., and were manifestly an integral portion of the Southern Confederacy Army. They were seen riding on horses and mules, driving wagons, riding on caissons, in ambulances, with the staff of generals, and promiscuously mixed up with all the rebel horde."[35]

Even from one of the strongest voices for the cause of abolition came from former slave Frederick Douglass in an essay he produced. From his *Douglass Monthly*, September 1861, he stated, "It is now pretty well established, that there are at the present moment many colored men in the Confederate army doing duty not only as cooks, servants and laborers, but as real soldiers, having muskets on their shoulders, and bullets in their pockets, ready to shoot down loyal troops, and do all that soldiers may to destroy the Federal government and build up that of the traitors and rebels. There were such soldiers at Manassas, and they are probably there still. There is a Negro in the army as well as in the fence, and our government is likely to find it out before the war comes to an end. That the Negroes are numerous in the rebel army, and do for that army its heaviest work,

is beyond question. They have been the chief laborers upon those temporary defenses in which the rebels have been able to mow down our men. Negroes helped to build the batteries at Charleston. They relieve their gentlemanly and military masters from the stiffening drudgery of the camp, and devote them to the nimble and dexterous use of arms.

---

[35]Report of Lewis H. Steiner (New York: Anson D. F. Randolph, 1862), 10-11.

Rising above vulgar prejudice, the slaveholding rebel accepts the aid of the black man as readily as that of any other. If a bad cause can do this, why should a good cause be less wisely conducted? We insist upon it, that one black regiment in such a war as this is, without being any more brave and orderly, would be worth to the government more than two of any other; and that, while the government continues to refuse the aid of colored men, thus alienating them from the national cause, and giving the rebels the advantage of them, it will not deserve better fortunes than it has thus far experienced. — Men in earnest don't fight with one hand, when they might fight with two, and a man drowning would not refuse to be saved even by a colored hand."[36]

The question which really needs to be asked is, "why would Negroes (slave or free) seek to support the Confederacy, whether a cook or a soldier or anything between?" Would we dare think blacks were fighting in order to preserve slavery. Mr. Wesley gives us a clue, "To the majority of the Negroes, as to all the South, the invading armies of the Union seemed to be ruthlessly attacking independent States, invading the beloved homeland and trampling upon all that these men held dear."[37]

## Hispanics in The Confederacy

Another group of men and women of color who served in the Confederate cause were from the Hispanic peoples. Texas, Florida and Louisiana had large Hispanic populations who enlisted to defend their homeland. Hispanics were well represented in the Confederate Army, such as the 6th Missouri Infantry Regiment, the 55th Alabama Infantry Regiment, the 2nd Texas Mounted Rifles, the 1st Florida Cavalry Regiment and the 33rd Texas Cavalry Regiment, commanded by Colonel Santos Benavides, the highest ranking Hispanic officer on the Confederate side. Benavides was born in Laredo and was the great-great-grandson of Tomás Sánchez de la Barrera y Garza, the founder of Laredo.[38] When Texas seceded from the Union, Benavides and his brothers supported

---

[36]Brenda Chambers McKean, *Blood and War At My Doorstep*, Vol 2 (Xlibris Corporation, 2011) 869.

[37]Charles H. Wesley, *The Employment of Negroes As Soldiers in the Confederate Army* (*The Journal of Negro History* Volume IV, July, No. 3, 1919), 241.

[38]Ivan A. Castro, *100 Hispanics You Should Know* (Libraries Unlimited, 2006), 32.

the Confederacy, whose states' rights principles were so close to their own thinking concerning the upper Rio Grande area. Perhaps Colonel Benavides greatest military triumph was his defense of his hometown of Laredo on March 19, 1864, with 42 troops against 200 Union soldiers.[39] His regiment put down various anti-Confederate mutinies and safeguarded the safe passage of cotton to the Mexican port of Matamoros after the Northern Army occupied Brownsville in 1864. Although poorly equipped and underfed, the 33rd never lost a battle.

Benavides

But there were other Hispanics who served in the Confederate Army. Those of the Louisiana Zouaves Battalion, the Spanish Legion of the European Brigade, and the Spanish Guard of Mobile, Alabama, all of which, fought for the rebel cause — states' rights. It has been estimated about 13,000 Hispanics served in the ranks of the Confederacy. There were at least 3,000 Mexicans in Texas alone who joined the Confederate Army. Mexicans who fought for the Confederacy outnumbered the amount of Mexicans fighting for the Union by a ratio of three to one.

Buford/Velasquez

But there were also Hispanic women who were represented in the ranks. Cuban-born on June 26, 1842, Loretta Janeta Velasquez was one of the most famous woman soldiers. In 1849, she was sent to school in New Orleans, where she resided with her aunt. At the age of 14, she eloped with an officer in the Texas army. When Texas seceded from the Union in 1861, her husband joined the Confederate army and Velazquez pleaded with him to allow her to join him. Undiscouraged by her husband's refusal, Velazquez had a lieutenant's uniform made and disguised her as a man, taking the name Harry T. Buford.[40] Velazquez fought at

[39]Ibid, 32.
[40]C.J. Worthington, Editor, *The Woman In Battle: A Narrative of the Exploits, Adventure, and Travels of Madame Loretta Janeta Velasquez, Otherwise Known As Harry T. Buford, Confederate States Army* (Hartford: T. Belknap, 1876), 61.

Sanchez

First Manassas, Ball's Bluff and Fort Pillow. In time, her gender was discovered and she was discharged. She would soon rejoined and fight again at the Battle of Shiloh. Once again discovered, she ended her military career working as a Confederate spy. As a spy, Velazquez was able to travel freely in both the South and the North; working in both male and female disguises and once again, for the rebel cause — states' rights.

Then there was the Sanchez family, who moved to Florida from Cuba. The Sanchez family included an ailing father, an invalid mother, a son who served in the Confederate army and three daughters; Panchita, Lola and Eugenia, who would become Confederate spies who were never caught. In time their father would be arrested for his support of the Confederacy. The sisters would respond by relaying information which led to the ambush of a Union gunboat and the Battle of Braddock's Farm. This resulted in a Confederate victory due to the information given by the Sanchez sisters. More than that, it resulted in the destruction and capture of part of the 17th Connecticut Infantry on February 15, 1865.[41]

## Indians (Native Americans) In the Confederacy

Another group of men of color who served in the Confederate cause were Native-Americans. Confederate units of Indian Territory consisted of Native Americans from the Five Civilized Tribes: the Cherokee, the Chickasaw, the Choctaw, the Creek and the Seminole nations.[42] These Indian tribes signed treaties with and served the Confederacy, beginning in the summer of 1861. In late fall of 1861, Chief John Ross of the Cherokees abandoned his original stance of neutrality and also signed the treaty with the Confederacy. In

Ross

---

[41]John O'Donnell-Rosales, *Hispanic Confederates* (Clearfield, 3 edition, 2009), 128-129.
[42]Clarissa Confer, *The Cherokee Nation in the Civil War* (University of Oklahoma Press, 2007), 4.

these treaties the Confederate government promised to assume federal obligations, protect tribes from invasion, and invited Indian representation in the Confederate Congress. About 15,000 American Indians served in the Confederacy Army.

Cooper

By the end of the war, the Confederate troops of the Indian Territory were organized into a division of two brigades. The first brigade was commanded by Brigadier General Douglas H. Cooper composed of Indian regiments and battalions and of troops of Texas Cavalry and rangers. The second was commanded by Lieutenant Colonel Tandy Walker of the Second Indian Cavalry Brigade consisting of Choctaw and Chickasaw troops and a reserve unit of Caddo Indians.

Walker

Brigadier General Stand Watie, a Cherokee, commanded all the Indian units not in the Choctaw Brigade. The flag he used was that of the 1st National Flag, which was introduced to the Cherokee Nation by Albert Pike when one was given to the people on October 7, 1861, at Park Hill, Indian Territory. This flag was described from a *Fort Smith Times* reporter "The Confederate Flag floats over our camp. In its blue field are the eleven white stars, in a circle, and inside that circle the commissioner has placed four small red stars, forming the four extremities of a passion cross — for the four nations, the Choctaws, Chickasaws, Creeks and Seminoles, in token that these Christian tribes of red men are encircled by our protection, and are with and of us. When, if ever, we deem it fit to treat with the Cherokees, a fifth red star will form the centre of the cross ..." Finally, in our history books, General Watie would be known as the last Confederate general in the field to surrender. He did this on June 23, 1865, at Doaksville, Choctaw Nation.

Watie

These are the Indian Tribal units which were commissioned and fought with the Confederate States of America in the Indian Territory:

General Stand Watie's flag

### Cherokee Nation

First Cherokee Mounted Rifles
First Regiment of Cherokee Mounted Volunteers
Second Regiment of Cherokee Mounted Volunteers
Cherokee Regiment [Special Services,] CSA
Third Cherokee Regiment of Volunteer Cavalry
First Cherokee Battalion of Partisan Rangers
First Squadron of Cherokee Mounted Volunteers
Cherokee Special Services Battalion
Scales' Battalion of Cherokee Cavalry
Meyer's Battalion of Cherokee Cavalry
Cherokee Battalion of Infantry
Second Cherokee Artillery

### Creek Nation

First Regiment Creek Mounted Volunteers
Second Regiment Creek Mounted Volunteers
First Battalion Creek Confederate Cavalry

## Seminole Nation

First Battalion Seminole Mounted Volunteers
First Regiment Seminole Mounted Volunteers

## Chickasaw Nation

First Regiment of Chickasaw Infantry
First Regiment of Chickasaw Cavalry
First Battalion of Chickasaw Cavalry
Shecoe's Chickasaw Battalion of Mounted Volunteers

## Choctaw Nation

First Regiment Choctaw & Chickasaw Mounted Rifles
First Regiment of Choctaw Mounted Rifles
Deneale's Regiment of Choctaw Warriors
Second Regiment of Choctaw Cavalry
Third Regiment of Choctaw Cavalry
Folsom's Battalion of Choctaw Mounted Rifles
Capt. John Wilkin's Company of Choctaw Infantry

*So, let it be said again — the North was not the only ones with men and women of color who fought in the War Between the States.*

*Another Look At Six Myths In The Lost Cause — Richard Lee Montgomery*

# ☞ Myth # 5

## It Was the South Who Were the Racists

Yes, there were those in the South who were racist, BUT, the North had their racists as well. To begin with, the *Civil War*, as the North called it, was not originally structured as a war to free the slaves. In its early years, President Abraham Lincoln promised not to impose abolitionist goals on the South. But Lincoln did become desperate to keep border states like Kentucky and Maryland loyal to the Union. So, as a politician would do, Lincoln took steps to make the war explicitly about slavery. So again, as a politician, Lincoln goes before an audience and gives a speech on September 22, 1862, called the "Preliminary Emancipation Proclamation." Lincoln started this speech by saying, "That on the first day of January, in the year of our Lord one thousand eight hundred and sixty-three, all

Preliminary
Proclamation

persons held as slaves within any State, or designated part of a State, the people whereof shall then be in rebellion against the United States shall be then, thenceforward, and forever free."[43]

This proclamation warned the Confederate states that if they remained in rebellion against the United States on January 1, 1863, Lincoln, as commander-in-chief, would on that day declare all slaves to be free in areas under Confederate control. It behooves us to ask the

---

[43]James Bryce, *Speeches and Letters of Abraham Lincoln*, 1832-1865 (London : J. M. Dent & Company, 1894), 202.

**New York Draft Riots**

question, "Why did Lincoln wait until now to free slaves and for that matter, only freeing those in the 'rebellious states.'" This proclamation was the first of two executive orders which make up the "Emancipation Proclamation" and it changed the nature of the War Between The States. Already stated in Myth #1, the reason to invade the South was now, not about money or the tax revenue the North needed from South, it was about freeing slaves, but only in the South.

But even if the true intent of the North was to free all slaves, there was still a great deal of racism in the North and with it, violence and even death. Perhaps the most recognized is the draft riots in New York in July of 1863. In 1863, from July 13th to the 17th, literally, terror reigned in the streets of New York. Armed white mobs protested the first Federal conscription (draft) because it threatened the manufacturing and commercial centers. At the start, it began as a demonstration against the draft and Abraham Lincoln's Republican administration. Then it rapidly metamorphosed into some of the bloodiest race riots which left at least 11 black men lynched. The violence by longshoremen against black men was especially fierce in the shipyard. During the riots, landlords feared their buildings would be destroyed and had their black tenants forced from their homes. As a result of the violence against blacks, hundreds left New York. By 1865 the total black population had dropped to under 10,000, the lowest it had been since 1820. Even New York historian Edward Robb Ellis wrote, "The Draft Riots ... stand as the most brutal, tragic, and shameful episode in the entire history of New York City. Politicians encouraged mob violence. Law and order broke down. Mobs seized control of America's largest city. Innocents were tortured and slaughtered [and] the Union army was weakened."[44]

---

[44]John H. Hewitt, *Protest and Progress: New York's First Black Episcopal Church Fights Racism* (Taylor & Francis, 2000) 128.

Perhaps we need to be reminded of the backdrop to these riots in New York City. As already stated in Myth #1, the slave trade was booming in New York City in the years just before the War Between the States. Horace Greeley even called the city a "nest of slave pirates."[45] The approximately 12,500 blacks in the city faced blatant discrimination. Segregation was common — blacks were excluded from white churches and theaters. This is simply not what we hear today from the mouths of most historians. The implications given to us today, if not the blatant teaching, are it was the South who was the racist.

Even during the Reconstruction period following the war, it is true there were "black codes" established so the local "whites" might control the local governments once again. But rarely are we told about the "black codes" which were established long before they existed in any Southern state, and to top it off, these codes were supported by many of the same Northern politicians who voted for the Fourteenth Amendment in July 9, 1868.

In the Revised Code of Indiana in 1862 stated "Negroes and mulattos are not allowed to come into the state," forbade the consummation of legal contracts with "Negroes and mulattos." It also imposed a $500 fine on anyone who employed a black person and forbade interracial marriage. It even had as a law that forbade blacks from testifying in court against white persons.[46]

Trumbull

Of all places, in the state of Illinois, the "land of Lincoln" added almost identical restrictions in their "black codes" in 1848. Later Senator Lyman Trumbull of Illinois, chairman of the Senate Judiciary Committee and a close friend of Abraham Lincoln's, confessed in July 1862 "there is a very great aversion in the West — I know it to be so in my state — against having free Negroes come among us. Our people want nothing to do with the Negro."[47] I suppose

[45]Ron Soodalter, *Hanging Captain Gordon: The Life and Trial of an American Slave Trader* (Simon and Schuster, 2010) 79.
[46]Richard Franklin Bensel, *Yankee Leviathan: The Origins of Central State Authority in America, 1859-1877* (Cambridge: Cambridge University Press, 1990), 62.
[47]LaWanda C. Fenlason Cox and Donald G. Nieman, *Freedom, Racism, and Reconstruction: Collected Writings of LaWanda Cox* (University of Georgia Press, 1997), 338.

it would go without saying that Trumbull supported the Illinois' "black codes," but if there is any doubt, he did.

Northern newspapers revealed their racial convictions:

*The Niles* (Michigan) *Republican*, March 30, 1861: "this government was made for the benefit of the white race ... and not for Negroes"

*Boston Daily Courier*, September 24, 1860: "we believe the mulatto to be inferior in capacity, character, and organization to the full-blooded black, and still farther below the standard of the white races."

The *Philadelphia Daily News*, November 22, 1860: "It is neither for the good of the colored race nor of our own that they should continue to dwell among us to any considerable extant. The two races can never exist in conjunction except as superior and inferior ... The African is naturally the inferior race."

The *Providence Daily Post*, February 2, 1861: "We have no more right to meddle with slavery in Georgia, than we have to meddle with monarchy in Europe ..."

*The Columbus* (Ohio) *Crisis*, February 7, 1861: "we are not Abolitionists nor in favor of Negro equality."

*The New York Herald*, March 7, 1861: "The immense increase in the numbers (of slaves) within so short a time speaks for the good treatment and happy, contented lot of the slaves. They are comfortably fed, housed and clothed, and seldom or never overworked."

Abraham Lincoln, in 1862 sent a letter to the *New York Tribune* editor Horace Greeley: "My paramount object in this struggle is to save the Union, and is not either to save or to destroy slavery. If I could save the Union without freeing any slave I would do it; and if I could save it by freeing some and leaving others alone I would also do that. What I do about slavery, and the colored race, I do because I believe it helps to save the Union."

It all boils down to what Alexis de Tocqueville wrote in his book,

*Democracy in America*, in which he was convinced that racial prejudice was stronger in the North than it was in the South. He says, "The prejudice of race appears to be stronger in the states that have abolished slavery than in those where it still exists."[48]

Tocqueville

Another interesting point which deserves attention, if the North was so set on bringing justice to all peoples of color, why did the Union government, after the War Between the States, send General's Sherman, Sheridan and Custer to the West to bring genocide to the Native Americans? It only took three months after the surrender of the Army of Northern Virginia by General Robert E. Lee, General Sherman was put in charge of the Military District of the Missouri, which was all land west of the Mississippi, and then was given the assignment to eradicate the Plains Indians in order to make way for the federally subsidized transcontinental railroad. In his book, *The Real Lincoln*, Thomas DiLorenzo's points out Abraham Lincoln and the Republican Party had a twisted view of "all men are equal."

The eradication of the Plains Indians was yet another subsidy to the railroad industry, albeit an indirect one. Rather than paying for rights of way across Indian lands, as James J. Hill's nonsubsidized Great Northern Railroad did, the government-subsidized Union Pacific and Central Pacific Railroads got the government to either kill or place on reservations every last Indian by 1890.

Sherman instructed his army that "during an assault [on an Indian village] the soldiers cannot pause to distinguish between male and female, or even discriminate as to age. As long as resistance is made, death must be meted out." As Sherman biographer John Marszalek wrote, "Sherman viewed Indians as he viewed recalcitrant Southerners during the war and newly freed people after: resisters to the legitimate forces of an orderly society." Of course, the chaos of entire Indian villages, women and children included, being wiped out by federal artillery is hardly an "orderly" scene....

---

[48]Alexis de Tocqueville, *Democracy in America*, Volume 1 (London: Longmans, Green, and Company, 1889), 364.

Sheridan

Sherman

Custer

Sherman and Sheridan purposely planned their raids during the winter months when they knew entire families would be together. They killed all the animals as well as the people, ensuring that any survivors would not survive for very long....

The fact the war against the Plains Indians began just three months after Lee's surrender calls into question yet again the notion that racial injustices in the South were the primary motivation for Northerners' willingness to wage such a long and destructive war. No political party purporting to be sensitive to racial injustice could possibly have even contemplated doing to the Indians what the United States government did to them.

Both the Southern Confederates and the Indians stood in the way of the Whig/Republican dream of a North American economic empire, complete with a subsidized transcontinental railroad, a nationalized banking system and protectionist tariffs. Consequently, both groups were conquered and subjugated by the most violent means.[49]

*It's a simple conclusion — racism in the North could be found before, during and after the War Between the States. So, it is not true the racists were only in the South because racism existed both in the North and the South.*

---

[49]Thomas DiLorenzo's, *The Real Lincoln: A New Look at Abraham Lincoln, His Agenda, and an Unnecessary War* (Paperback Edition, New York: Three Rivers Press, 2003), 220-223.

# Myth # 6

## God Was On The Side of the North

To say "God was on the side of the North" can easily be the conclusion of many because that's the normal way to think. After all, the North won the war. Certainly many in the North felt God was on their side, but then, there were many in the South who felt the same way. Many ministers on both sides went so far as to proclaim God had ordained the war and they were themselves

St. John's Church

God's "chosen people." You could hear that message from the pulpit, both in the North and the South. With the South's triumph in the war's first major battle at First Manassas on Sunday, July 21, 1861, sermons were preached that day about God's providence leading them to victory. In Richmond, Virginia, at St. John's (Episcopal) Church, William C. Butler declared:

"God has given us of the South today a fresh and golden opportunity — and so a most solemn command — to realize that form of government in which the just, constitutional rights of each and all are guaranteed to each and all.… He has placed us in the front rank of the most marked epochs of the world's history. He has placed in our hands a commission which we can faithfully execute only by holy, individual self-consecration to all of God's plans."[50]

Perhaps what is interesting about this particular church is that on March 23, 1775, a meeting of the Colony delegates at the Second Vir-

---

[50]Randall M. Miller, Harry S. Stout, Charles Reagan Wilson, *Religion and the American Civil War* (Oxford University Press, 1998), 322-323.

ginia Convention in Richmond saw Patrick Henry deliver his famous "Give me Liberty or give me death" speech. So it would be easy for Southerners to express this kind of mind-set, that God was going to lead them to victory.

**Howe**

While sermons were used to express their regional loyalties, North or South, songs were mighty tools as well. Perhaps Henry Frederic Reddall says it best, when giving us the balanced picture of the patriotic songs that were sung: "The sound of *John Brown's Body* and Mrs. Howe's noble *Battle Hymn of the Republic* echoed on every hilltop and in every valley where our soldiers marched and battled in the civil war; while *Dixie, The Bonnie Blue Flag* and *Maryland, My Maryland*, re-sounded back defiant strains from the Southern camps.

Thus music and song, appealing as they do strongly to the deep emotions of strong men, as well as of gentle women and little children, have a serious use in the most momentous struggles, and sometimes produce grave changes in the destinies of nations and continents."[51]

As a prominent American abolitionist, social activist, poet, and the author of *The Battle Hymn of the Republic*, Julia Ward Howe used the music from the song *John Brown's Body*, written around 1856 by William Steffe, to write her famous lyrics in November 1861 and was first published in *The Atlantic Monthly* in February 1862. Thus, we have *The Battle Hymn of the Republic*. It was in this song Howe applied the judgment of the "day of the Lord" to the destruction of the Southern armies by the North. This became their rally song believing God would lead them to victory.

In her short biography of Julia Ward Howe, Mary R. Parkman writes this about the influence of the *The Battle Hymn of the Republic*:

"And so the "nation's song" was born. How did it come to pass that the people knew it as their own? When it appeared in *The Atlantic*

---

[51]Henry Frederic Reddall, *Songs That Never Die* (New York: W. J. Holland, 1894), 75.

*Monthly* it called forth little comment; the days gave small chance for the poetry of words. But some poets in the real world of deeds had seen it the people who were fighting on the nation's battlefields. And again and again it was sung and chanted as a prayer before battle and a trumpet-call to action."[52]

Then there was the South's anthem, *Dixie*. One theory credits Ohio-born Daniel Decatur Emmett with the song's composition, however many other people have claimed to have composed *Dixie*, even during Emmett's lifetime. This song premiered in the black-face minstrel shows[53] of the 1850s and quickly grew famous across the United States. However, *Dixie* is best known as the song adopted by the Confederacy and for this very reason; Emmett was ostracized in the North for writing a song associated with the South. Another theory of the origin of the name *Dixie* is that the old $10 Louisiana notes were known as "dixies," and the Louisiana region became known in slang as Dixie Land. This term was later expanded to include the rest of the South. But what's important here, is that this catchy tune soon turned into one of the most popular patriotic songs in the Confederacy. It became their rally song built on the idea God was going to lead them to victory.

This song was known long before the war, but when the struggle began it was the means of expressing Southern sentiments exclusively. It became purely a sectional song, though prior to the war the tune was heard quite frequently throughout the North. The song was written by General Albert Pike, a native of Massachusetts, but a general in the Southern army. Many a time *Dixie Land* was heard in the still of the evening as it came from the Southern camps, but usually it was answered by Northern bands playing *Yankee Doodle*.[54]

---

[52]Mary R. Parkman, *Heroines Of Service* (New York: The Century Co., 1921), 145.

[53]Minstrel Shows: a medieval wandering musician who performed songs or recited poetry with instrumental accompaniment. Here, in this setting, it refers to a troupe of performers in black-face who create a stereotyped caricature of a black person.

[54]S. Brainards' Sons, *Our War Song: North and South* (Cleveland: S. Brainards' Sons, 1887), 10-11.

Another thought, if God was on the side of the North, then there needs to be an explanation of how God showed Himself on both sides of the war, with revival braking out in the camps of the Yankees and the Confederates. It has been speculated that in the Union Army, between 100,000 and 200,000 soldiers were converted and in the Confederate Army, approximately 150,000 troops converted to Christ. It has been suggested only 10 percent of all *Civil War* soldiers experienced conversions during the conflict.

In his book, *Both Prayed to the Same God: Religion and Faith in the American Civil War*, Robert J. Miller gives us a glimpse of the spiritual revival taking root in the Northern troops:

For the larger, more culturally diverse Union troops, revivalism was more gradual and steady, perhaps less "explosive" than the South. While the reality and proximity of death did motivate them, revivalism seemed more connected to the overall progress they were making in the war, giving them the encouragement needed to continue the war efforts. "The revivals gained force as the war's tempo accelerated and the soldiers felt themselves carried toward victory, and they thus tapped into the greater reservoir of emotions that the conflicted inspired."

A paragraph later, "As with the South, scattered revivals among Union troops began sporadically in 1862, grew rapidly throughout 1863, and reached a high in the winter of 1863-1864. Northern soldiers who had earlier dealt with "a tide of irreligion" (in the words of General Robert McAllister), now seemed to adopted a more reflective and religious attitude, seeking further strengthening (spiritually and materially) for the battles ahead. The religious enthusiasm of the Army of the Potomac led them to build many chapels and hold frequent prayer meetings. Black troops in the Atlantic coast garrisons also experienced a surge of spiritual fervor."[55]

At the Battle of Chattanooga in the fall and in the winter of 1863, the Union Army was deluged by a strong Confederate force. It was during this period that revival ensued and subsequently was called the

---

[55]Robert J. Miller, *Both Prayed to the Same God: Religion and Faith in the American Civil War* (Lexington Books, 2007), 123.

"Great Revival." Even though records of this happening were best documented by General Lee's Army of Northern Virginia, it is important to know that revival took place in both Northern and Southern Armies in both the Virginia and the Tennessee theaters of the war. It was during the Battle of Chattanooga that the Union soldiers were deeply affected by the revival, and many attributed their surprising victory over the Confederates as "a visible interposition of God."[56]

Lee

However, this "Great Revival" occurred among General Robert E. Lee's forces in the fall of 1863 and winter of 1864. Some 7,000 soldiers were converted. Sometimes preaching and praying continued 24 hours a day, and chapels couldn't hold the soldiers who wanted to get inside. Specifically in the Army of Northern Virginia in 1864, boasted 15 chapels. One chapel was built by the Army of the Tennessee and seated more than 1,000 soldiers. Of special note, Generals Robert E. Lee and Thomas "Stonewall" Jackson did all within their power to encourage the spreading of the Gospel

Jackson

in the Army of Northern Virginia. General Jackson would encourage the troops to keep the Sabbath holy and to attend worship services. He would even try to avoid battle on the Sabbath and if it was not possible,

General Jackson would try to set aside a day of rest following the battle. For General Jackson, he was a man of prayer. He would pray both before and during battle. He always acknowledged God as the author of his military victories.

According to J. William Jones, a Southern Baptist Confederate Chaplain, reported that nearly every Confederate brigade was affected by revival. Night after night troops participated in prayer meetings and listened to sermons on the Gospel message. Meetings

Jones

---

[56]Bruce Catton, *A Stillness at Appomattox* (Garden City, New York: Doubleday & Company, 1953), 187.

**Garland**

would end with soldiers coming forward to receive Christ or to pray. When a pond or river was nearby, the soldiers would frequently step forward for baptisms, regardless of how cold the weather was. Chaplain Jones wrote:

"My own brigade (Smith's, formerly Early's Virginia) was fortunately camped near Mt. Pisgah Baptist Church and a Methodist church in the lower part of Orange county, and Rev, J. P. Garland, of the Forty-ninth Virginia, Rev. Mr. Slaughter, of the Fifty-eighth Virginia, and myself united in holding meetings in both of these houses. We were fortunate in having at different times Rev. Dr. J. A. Broadus, Rev. F. M. Barker (the gifted, eloquent and lamented preacher who took in my tent the cold which resulted in his death), Rev. L. J. Haley and others to help us, and the work went graciously on until interrupted, but not stopped, by the 'Bristoe campaign.' There were 250 professions of conversion, and a revival among Christians, of the highest value."[57]

During the revival, Chaplain Jones also reported how "reading clubs" formed:

**Broadus**

"I have an old memorandum-book filled with names of soldiers from every state of the Confederacy who had applied to me for Bibles and Testaments, and some of the scenes I witnessed in my work of Bible and tract distribution are as fresh in my memory as if they had occurred on yesterday. I had a pair of large "saddle-bags" which I used to pack with tracts and religious newspapers, and with Bibles and Testaments when I had them, and besides this I would strap packages behind my saddle and on the pommel. Thus equipped I would sally forth, and as I drew near the camp someone would raise the cry, "Yonder comes the Bible and tract man," and such crowds would rush out to meet me, that frequently I would sit on my horse and distribute my supply before I could even get into the camp. But if I had Bibles or Testaments to distribute, the poor

---

[57]J. William Jones, *Christ In The Camp or Religion In Lee's Army* (Richmond, Va.: B. F. Johnson & Co.), 319.

fellows would crowd around and beg for them as earnestly as if they were golden guineas for free distribution. Yes, the word of God seemed to these brave men "more precious than gold — yea than much fine gold." The men were accustomed to form " reading clubs," not to read the light literature of the

**Prayer in Jackson's Camp**

day, but to read God's word, and not unfrequently have I seen groups of twenty-five or thirty gather around some good reader, who for several hours would read with clear voice selected portions of the Scriptures."[58]

So, now we come back to the statement, "God was on the side of the North." Both the North and the South had their rally songs which proved to do just that — unify their different convictions. Both the North and the South offered up their prayers before God believing God would lead them to victory. And both the North and the South experienced revivals, which then spurred the soldiers on to fight for victory and for the preachers to preach that God was leading their particular side. Robert J. Miller entitled his book the best possible name, *Both Prayed to the Same God: Religion and Faith in the American Civil War.*

***Indeed God was involved in showing Himself to both the North and the South — not just the North.***

---

[58]J. William Jones, *Christ In The Camp or Religion In Lee's Army* (Richmond, Va.: B. F. Johnson & Co.), 155.

*Another Look At Six Myths In The Lost Cause — Richard Lee Montgomery*

# Bibliography

## Books

*Abraham Lincoln: Speeches and Writings, 1832-1858*, (New York: Library of America, 1989).

Report of Lewis H. Steiner (New York: Anson D. F. Randolph, 1862).

*Some Ships of the Clipper Ship Era: Their Builders, Owners, and Captains*, (Boston, MA: Printed for the State Street Trust Company, 1913).

*The Sesquicentennial of Brown University, 1764-1914* (Printed By The University, 1915).

Adkins, Ray, *One Foggy Morning In Barbourville*, Kentucky (CreateSpace Independent Publishing Platform, 2008).

Alfriend, Frank H., *The Life of Jefferson Davis* (Cincinnati: Caxton Publishing House, 1868)

Basler, Roy P., *The Collected Works of Abraham Lincoln*, Volume 1, (Rutgers University Press, New Brunswich, New Jersey, 1953).

Bennett, Lerone Jr., *Forced into Glory: Abraham Lincoln's White Dream*, (Johnson Publishing Company, Inc, 2007).

Bensel, Richard Franklin, *Yankee Leviathan: The Origins of Central State Authority in America, 1859-1877* (Cambridge: Cambridge University Press, 1990).

Brainards' Sons, *Our War Song: North and South* (Cleveland: S. Brainards' Sons, 1887).

Bryce, James, *Speeches and Letters of Abraham Lincoln, 1832-1865* (London : J. M. Dent & Company, 1894).

Cannon, Jr., Devereaux D., *The Flags of the Confederacy*, (St. Lukes Press and Broadfoot Publishing, 1988).

Catton, Bruce, *A Stillness at Appomattox* (Garden City, New York: Doubleday & Company, 1953).

Carey, Matthew Jr., *The Democratic Speaker's Hand Book*, (Cincinnati: Miami Print and Pub Company, 1868).

Castro, Ivan A., *100 Hispanics You Should Know* (Libraries Unlimited, 2006).

Confer, Clarissa, *The Cherokee Nation in the Civil War* (University of Oklahoma Press, 2007).

Coughtry, Jay, *The Notorious Triangle: Rhode Island and the African Slave Trade*, (Philadelphia, 1981).

Cox, LaWanda C. Fenlason and Nieman, Donald G., *Freedom, Racism, and Reconstruction: Collected Writings of LaWanda Cox* (University of Georgia Press, 1997), 338.

Deane, Charles, *The Connection of Massachusetts With Slavery And The Slave Trade*, (Worcester, Mass: Charles Hamilton,1886).

de Tocqueville, Alexis, *Democracy in America*, Volume 1 (London: Longmans, Green, and Company, 1889), 364.

DeWolf, Thomas Norman, I*nheriting the Trade: A Northern Family Confronts Its Legacy as the Largest Slave-Trading Dynasty in U.S. History* (Beacon Press, 2008).

DiLorenzo's, Thomas, *The Real Lincoln: A New Look at Abraham Lincoln, His Agenda, and an Unnecessary War* (Paperback Edition, New York: Three Rivers Press, 2003).

Dorsey, Christopher, *A Call to Arms: The Realities of Military Service for African Americans During the Civil War*, (Backintyme, 2007).

Greely, Horace, *The American Conflict*, Vol. 2 (Hartford: O. D. Case & Company, 1867).

Greene, Lorenzo Johnston, *The Negro in Colonial New England, 1620-1776* (N.Y.: Columbia University Press, 1942).

Hewitt, John H., *Protest and Progress: New York's First Black Episcopal Church Fights Racism* (Taylor & Francis, 2000) 128.

Howe, M. A. DeWolfe, *Home Letters of General Sherman*, (New York: C. Scribner's Sons, 1909).

Hume, Edgar Erskine, *The German Artist Who Designed the Confederate Flag and Uniform* (*The American-German Review*, August, 1940).

Inikor, Joseph E., *The Atlantic Slave Trade: Effects on Economies, Societies and Peoples in Africa, the Americas, and Europe*, (Duke University Press Books, 1992).

Jennings, Arthur H., Chairman, *The Gray Book*, (Gray Book Committee S.C.V., By Authority, and Under Auspices of The Sons of Confederate Veterans, 1920).

Jones, J. William, *Christ In The Camp or Religion In Lee's Army* (Richmond, Va.: B. F. Johnson & Co.).

Jordan, Ervin L., *Confederates and Afro-Yankees in Civil War Virginia* (University of Virginia, 1995).

Kellogg, J., *Confederate Women of Arkansas In The Civil War: 1861-1865* (The United Confederate Veterans of Arkansas, 1907).

Kennedy, Walter Donald, *Myths of American Slavery*, (Pelican Publishing; 1st Edition, 2003).

Lewis, Lloyd, *Sherman: Fighting Prophet*, (University of Nebraska Press, 1932).

Martin, Iain C., *The Quotable American Civil War*, (Lyons Press, 2008).

Mckean, Brenda Chambers, *Blood and War At My Doorstep*, Vol 2 (Xlibris Corporation, 2011).

McManus, Edgar J., *Black Bondage in the North* (N.Y.: Syracuse University Printing, 2002).

Miller, Randall M., Harry S. Stout, Charles Reagan Wilson, *Religion and the American Civil War* (Oxford University Press, 1998).

O'Donnell-Rosales, John, *Hispanic Confederates* (Clearfield, 3 edition, 2009).

Parkman, Mary R., *Heroines of Service* (New York: The Century Co., 1921).

Pierce, Edward Lillie, *Memoir and Letters of Charles Sumner*, Volume 4, (Boston: Roberts Brothers, 1894).

Randolph, Sarah Nicholas, *The Life of General Thomas J. Jackson* (Philadelphia: J. B. Lippincott & Co., 1876).

Reddall, Henry Frederic, *Songs That Never Die* (New York: W. J. Holland, 1894).

Soodalter, Ron, *Hanging Captain Gordon: The Life and Trial of an American Slave Trader* (Simon and Schuster, 2010) 79.

Wesley, Charles H., *The Employment Of Negroes As Soldiers In The Confederate Army* (*The Journal of Negro History* Volume IV, July, No. 3, 1919).

Worthington, C.J., Editor, *The Woman In Battle: A Narrative of the Exploits, Adventure, and Marvels of Madame Loretta Janeta Velasquez, Otherwise Known As Harry T. Buford, Confederate States Army* (Hartford: T. Belknap, 1876).

# Journals

*Southern Historical Society Papers*, Volume 24, 1876.

# Newspapers

"In Defense of His Confederate Pride," *St. Petersburg Times*, October 2007, retrieved March 22, 2011.

*Black Southerner Marching To D.C., Seeks Respect For Confederate Flag*, Sons of Confederate Veterans.

Moyer, Laura, "Rebel Re-Enactor With A Cause," *The Free Lance-Star*, June 30, 2002.

# Web

Adam Goodheart November 3, 2010. *New York Times.* or http://opinionator.blogs. nytimes.com/ 2010/11/03/a-slave-ship-in-new-york/

CPSIA information can be obtained at www.ICGtesting.com
Printed in the USA
LVOW05s0722220114

370463LV00003B/94/P